IT'S TIME TO EAT WHITE CHOCOLATE CHUNK COOKIES

It's Time to Eat WHITE CHOCOLATE CHUNK COOKIES

Walter the Educator

Silent King Books
A WhichHead Entertainment Imprint

Copyright © 2024 by Walter the Educator

All rights reserved. No part of this book may be reproduced in any manner whatsoever without written per- mission except in the case of brief quotations embodied in critical articles and reviews.

First Printing, 2024

Disclaimer

This book is a literary work; the story is not about specific persons, locations, situations, and/or circumstances unless mentioned in a historical context. Any resemblance to real persons, locations, situations, and/or circumstances is coincidental. This book is for entertainment and informational purposes only. The author and publisher offer this information without warranties expressed or implied. No matter the grounds, neither the author nor the publisher will be accountable for any losses, injuries, or other damages caused by the reader's use of this book. The use of this book acknowledges an understanding and acceptance of this disclaimer.

It's Time to Eat WHITE CHOCOLATE CHUNK COOKIES is a collectible early learning book by Walter the Educator suitable for all ages belonging to Walter the Educator's Time to Eat Book Series. Collect more books at WaltertheEducator.com

USE THE EXTRA SPACE TO TAKE NOTES AND DOCUMENT YOUR MEMORIES

WHITE CHOCOLATE CHUNK COOKIES

It's cookie time, oh what a sight,

It's Time to Eat
White Chocolate Chunk Cookies

White chocolate chunks so big and bright!

Soft and chewy, warm and sweet,

The perfect snack for us to eat.

The chunks are creamy, smooth, and fine,

Each bite feels like a little shine.

Golden edges, a tender middle,

This tasty treat solves any riddle!

The smell drifts out, it fills the air,

"Come to the kitchen!" the cookies declare.

With milk in hand, we gather 'round,

White chocolate joy in every sound.

A little nibble, a happy grin,

Let the cookie fun begin!

Each chunk surprises, so much to see,

A treasure hunt for you and me.

It's Time to Eat

White Chocolate Chunk Cookies

We count the chunks, one, two, three,

How many more? Let's look and see!

They're hidden deep, a creamy prize,

White chocolate chunks are a delight to find.

We'll share with friends, a bite for all,

Big cookies, small cookies, we'll have a ball.

It's fun to give, it's fun to share,

Cookies show how much we care.

One more bite, oh what a dream,

Cookies and chunks are the perfect team!

Each taste is cozy, warm, and right,

A snack so special, day or night.

Now crumbs are left, the plate is bare,

But cookie memories linger there.

It's Time to Eat White Chocolate Chunk Cookies

We'll bake again, another batch,

For White Chocolate Chunk, there's no match!

So here's to cookies, fresh and sweet,

A treat that's always hard to beat.

White chocolate chunks, we love you so,

The best of snacks, that's what we know!

The cookie jar is empty now,

.

But we'll refill it, we know how!

With dough to roll and chunks to toss,

It's Time to Eat

White Chocolate Chunk Cookies

White Chocolate Chunk, our baking boss!

ABOUT THE CREATOR

Walter the Educator is one of the pseudonyms for Walter Anderson. Formally educated in Chemistry, Business, and Education, he is an educator, an author, a diverse entrepreneur, and he is the son of a disabled war veteran. "Walter the Educator" shares his time between educating and creating. He holds interests and owns several creative projects that entertain, enlighten, enhance, and educate, hoping to inspire and motivate you. Follow, find new works, and stay up to date with Walter the Educator™

at WaltertheEducator.com

www.ingramcontent.com/pod-product-compliance
Lightning Source LLC
LaVergne TN
LVHW052016060526
838201LV00059B/4054